WHAT Are You Afraid Of?

What **ARE** You Afraid Of?

What Are **YOU** Afraid Of?

What Are You **AFRAID** Of?

What Are You Afraid **OF**?

By

Dr. Margaret Cochran

Life Is A Process of Becoming,

But It Is Not Always A Becoming Process

Prologue

I send you greetings Intrepid Seeker!

This book is an invitation, an invitation to the beginning of a journey.

However, this journey, like all worthy adventures, will not be without challenge.

And there will be many who will urge you, by attempting to make you afraid, not to take it.

It is a journey for awareness and intellectual and emotional balance in which you are endeavoring to know your <u>own</u> thoughts and feelings.

And one that will take you quite literally to another world.

For you see; things, people, decisions, actually life in general, will look completely different when you are not afraid and you are no longer controlled by those who use fear to manipulate you.

Bon chance!

And as always I wish you Wisdom, Productive Decision Making, Love and Magic!

Margaret Cochran

A Wise Man Once Said,

"Be Not Afraid",

But Mostly Nobody Listened.

You Know

It's Only The Things We Run From,

That Can Chase Us.

Are YOU

Afraid

Of Anything?

Are You Perhaps Afraid

Of Finding Out

What You Are <u>Really</u> Afraid Of?

Be Honest!

OK. Stop What You Are Doing Right Now.

Move Any Distractions, Mental Or Otherwise

Out Of The Way.

And, Ask Yourself,

What Am I Afraid Of, Really?

Make A List Of Your Fears Now.

Were You Surprised?

Pleased?

Did This Exercise Engender More Fear In You?

Or Less?

Now…

Why Do You Think,

And Why Do You Feel,

That You Are Afraid Of The Things

And People On Your List?

No Really,

Why?

Dig A Little Deeper.

You Can Do It.

Make A List Of Your Thoughts and Feelings Now

What Do You Think Of Your List?

How Do You Feel About Yourself

When You Read It?

Who Do You Become

When You Are Afraid?

Are You Happy?

Angry?

Defensive?

Brave?

Humorous?

Impatient?

Critical?

Cowering?

Violent?

What?

Maybe Sometimes You Are Afraid,

And You Don't

Recognize It As Such.

Fear Doesn't Always Manifest Itself

As

Sweaty Palms

And

A Pounding Pulse.

Sometimes It Looks Like Avoidance,

Minimization,

Rationalization,

Denial

And/Or

A Moment Of Vituperative Spew.

So Think About Some Times When You Were Afraid,

And

Write Down Who You Became,

And

What You Did.

Write Your Observations Down.

No, Don't Skip This Part,

Write Them Down!

There Is An Old Saying:

'Don't Work So Hard

For Your Money,

Make Your Money

Work Hard For You'.

Now, Substitute The Word Fear

For The Word Money

And Write The Saying Again.

Just About Now, Some Of You Will Be Saying,

"This Is Stupid!

I Don't Need To Write Down My Thoughts And

Feelings".

If you Truly Want To Change Them

Then, Yes, You Do.

You Have To Have The Courage To Own Your Fears
To Be Empowered Enough To Let Them Go Or Use
Them Differently.

Writing Things Down Helps You Do That.

The Written Word Helps To Concretize Ideas That We
Might Otherwise Dismiss Or Forget.

Your Fears And Feelings And Awareness Of Yourself
Are Far Too Important To Dismiss Or Forget.

So Write Them Down!

But,

If You Are Too Afraid To Face Your Fears For Now…

Just Admit It.

You Can Be Controlled

By Fear

As Long As You Need,

Or Want To Be.

The Universe Is Infinitely Patient.

But,

Before You Give Up,

If You Are So Inclined,

I Want To Take This Opportunity To Tell You

That It Isn't Really Necessary

To <u>Let</u> Fear Control Your Life.

Really!

OK,

You May Close The Book Now If You Wish.

But Don't Forget That You

Can Open It Again

Any Time YOU Are Ready.

Any Time YOU Are Ready!

Did I Mention

That

The Universe Is Infinitely Patient?

There Are Many Who are Interested In Keeping Us

Afraid; Employers, Schools, Churches, Politicians,

News Media and Television, among Others.

You Might Wonder Why Anyone Would Want Another Human Being To Feel Fear. Well, Of Course, The Answer Is Because Only 'They' Have The Answers Necessary To Make The Fear Go Away. All You Have To Do Is Think What 'They' Say, Vote As 'They' Say, Live Your Life As 'They' Say, And Everything Will Be 'Fine'. I Think That's Scary, Don't You?

One Important Technique For Keeping People Afraid Is Distraction.

Herman Goering, Who It Turns Out Was Not Only Among Hitler's Elite Within The Nazi Party But Also Somewhat Of A Political Scientist, Said, "But After All It Is The Leaders Of The Country That Determine The Policy And It Is Always A Simple Matter To Drag The People Along, Whether It Is A Democracy, Or A Fascist Dictatorship, Or A Parliament Or A Communist Dictatorship. …The People Can Always Be Brought To The Bidding Of The Leaders. That Is Easy. All You Have To Do Is Tell Them They Are Being Attacked And Denounce The Pacifists For Lack Of Patriotism And Exposing The Country To Danger. It Works The Same Way In Any Country."

Truer Words Were Never Spoken!

Another Example Of Distraction Is How We Handle Certain Diseases. Specifically The Astronomical Increase In The Diagnosis Of Cancer In The World. Lots Of People Want You To Buy And Wear Cute Little Ribbons About Finding A Cure, But Nobody Wants You To Ask The Question Why Is The Cancer Rate So High? There Are Lots And Lots And Lots Of Institutions Who Don't Want You To Go There.

Do You Feel Afraid Right Now? Don't Be. You Have The Power To Change Everything If You Are Ready To Use Fear Constructively.

Speaking Of Fear…

Did You Know That Most Of The Stories Told On

So Called Reality TV Are Not Actually…

You Only See What The Editors And Producers Decide

Is Real.

Fortunately, This Isn't Reality TV.

And I Am Going To Tell You A Story,

<u>Unlike</u> Reality TV,

This Story Is True.

First Of All Though,

I'm Going To Tell You

Something Funny And Amazing.

I Frequently Strike Terror In People's Hearts.

If You Saw Me In Person

You Would Know That I Am Hardly Intimidating;

But

I <u>Am</u> Scary.

Except Not Really.

You See, People Think It's Me They Are Afraid Of

But,

It's Really Themselves And The Things On Their List.

A Good Psychotherapist Holds Up A Mirror.

Those Of Us Who Are Brave Enough, Look Into That

Mirror.

And,

Sometimes We Like What We See

And

Sometimes Not.

What We See, Might Make Us Afraid

And

Since The Therapist Is The One Holding The Mirror…

Well, You Get The Gist.

Anyway,

Many People Have Lived With Fear So Long

That They

Don't Know How To Live Without It.

In Fact,

This Is A <u>Huge</u> Problem!

Many People Who Have Difficulties With

Relationships

Or Work,

Trouble With Their Children,

Or

Who Suffer From Anxiety,

Depression

And/Or

AD/HD,

Among Other Things - Don't Get Help,

Because They Are Afraid.

When People In Pain Do Get Help,

They Often Need Support In Knowing

How To Feel And Be

Without Fear As Their Constant Companion.

But Often They Are Afraid Of That Help.

Have You Ever Been Afraid To Ask A Question Or To

Seek Help?

Write Down What You Are Afraid Of And Why You

Didn't Ask For Assistance.

Now,

For The Long Awaited

TRUE Story…

Once Upon A Time,

Quite Recently In Fact…

There Was A Wonderful Woman

And...

She Was Smart, Funny And Cute,

As Well As Being

Anxious, Fearful And Depressed.

In Fact She Had Been Anxious, Fearful And Depressed

For So Long

That She Didn't Know Any Other Way To Be.

She Thought Feeling Bad

Was Normal!

She Was Afraid That Having The Diseases Of

Anxiety And Depression Meant That

There Was Something

Wrong With Her Character,

That Somehow She Was Weak Or Bad.

So She Just Accepted

Things As They Were,

And Didn't Talk Much

About How She Felt.

Although She Didn't Realize It

Consciously

At The Time,

She Helped Alleviate Some Of Her Discomfort By

Self Medicating

With Nicotine.

Everyday She Smoked Two Or Three Cigarettes.

"It's Not That Many," She Would Say.

Then, One Day She Was Diagnosed

With Cancer.

Not Lung Cancer Mind You.

But, Cancer Just The Same.

Well, As You Might Guess

Having Cancer

Made Her Anxiety And Depression Worse.

But, In Her Mind,

Because She Had Cancer

It Was Now "OK"

To Ask For Help.

In Fact, She Was Told,

It Was An Important Part

Of Getting Well.

And So,

In Addition To Her Chemotherapy

And

Radiation Therapy,

She Had Psychotherapy

And She Took Medication For Her

Anxiety and Depression.

She Felt It Really Helped Her.

In Fact,

She Would Often Say

That She Didn't Know What

She Would Have Done Without Them.

And, She Quit Smoking!

She Fought Her Cancer

And

She Got Well!

When Her Cancer Was In

Remission Though

Suddenly, Somehow,

It Was Not OK To Take The Medicine For Her Anxiety

And Depression

And Go To Therapy

Any More.

So She Stopped Them Both.

Her Anxiety

And Depression

Returned

And, She Started Self Medicating With Nicotine Again.

The Return Of Her Depression And Anxiety

Was Slow And Insidious.

So, She Couldn't Figure Out Why She Wanted To Start

Smoking Again.

She Would Say, "I Know It's Bad For Me,

But I Just Can't Seem To Stop".

She Was Afraid.

She Was Afraid Of Asking For Help,

She Was Afraid To Quit Smoking,

She Was Afraid Of Cancer,

She Was Afraid To Live With Anxiety And Depression,

And She Was Afraid To Die.

She Was Very, Very Afraid.

No One Ever Explained To Her

That It Isn't Necessary Or Normal

To Feel Bad All The Time.

"But", She Would Say, "In A Funny Way I Felt The

Best I've Ever Felt When I Was Sick With Cancer".

Two Years Later,

She Got Sick Again.

She Died Of Lung Cancer

At Age 49.

The Fear And The Cancer Won.

Sad.

Not Everyone Has

Depression And Anxiety

Like The Wonderful Woman In Our Story.

But Most Of Us Have Fears

Of One Kind Or Another.

Fear Can Stop You

From

Taking Care Of Yourself

Or

Taking Important Life Changing Risks.

Or

From Falling In Love

Or

Making An Emotional Commitment…

Or

Choosing To Start A Family

Or

Protecting Yourself And Your Children From

Emotional or Physical Violence

Or

Asking For A Raise

Or

Treating An Addiction

Or

Getting An Education

Or…

What Have You Let Fear Stop You From Doing?

You Know The Drill By Now, Make Your List!

So, How Was That For You?

What Did You Learn?

Fear Can Be

A Wonderful Teacher

Or

A Horrible Master.

If You Let It,

Fear Can Show You A Lot About Yourself,

Who You Really Are,

What You Really Want,

And What And Whom You Really Value.

Or,

It Can Control

And Destroy

Your Life.

Imagine

Being Able To Feel Your Worst Fears

And

Use Them

To Energize You

To Do Or Be What You Want,

Instead Of Worrying About Them.

Worrying,

After All,

Is Praying For

What You Don't Want.

So What Now,

You Might Ask?

What Am I To

Do

With What I Know About

Fear?

Well,

That's Up To

You

Of Course.

But I'll Leave You

With This…

If You Get Stuck

In A Fearful Place, Remember To…

Identify Your Fear And Embrace It. Fear Is Not Something To Be Gotten Rid Of But Something To Be Harnessed And Used To Your Advantage.

When You Have Named Your Fear Let It Guide You

To WHAT YOU <u>DO</u> WANT TO HAPPEN.

Make A Plan That Is Broken Down Into Small Easy To Achieve Steps Outlining How You Can Move Toward Your Goals And Dreams. Do Not Waste Time Avoiding Fear, Remember To Let It Work Hard For You.

Ask For Help. And If You Feel Afraid To Ask For

Help, Which Would Manifest Itself As Anger,

Avoidance, Anxiety Or A 'Rafting Trip On The River

Of Denial'. Then Drag Yourself Kicking And

Screaming To The Nearest Professional Helper. That

Person May Be A Physician, A Psychotherapist, Clergy,

Body Worker, Life Coach, Favorite Professor, Parent,

Whomever.

Do It!

Spend Time Around Positive, Fearless People. Read And Listen To Inspirational Material That Doesn't Tell You What To Think But <u>How</u> To Think.

Visualize Your 'Now' And Your 'Tomorrow' The Way You Want Them To Be.

You Will Draw To You The People And Events That

Reflect Who You Are Internally. If You Don't Like The

People You Are With Or The Circumstances You Find

Yourself In And You Are Afraid To Make Changes

You Know The Answer.

Make A Plan!

Get Help!

If You Find Yourself Wanting To Cling To The
Familiar No Matter How Dysfunctional Or Painful It Is,
Follow The Steps I Have Mentioned, And If You Get
Stuck.

Ask For Help!

When You Do Let Go Of Toxic, Unnecessary Things

Or People, YOU WILL NOT BE DEPLETED.

You Will BE MAKING ROOM FOR MORE

DESIRABLE PEOPLE AND THINGS TO COME

INTO YOUR LIFE.

A Balanced Life Is The Key To Living A Fearless

Existence.

Eat Well, Exercise, Rest And Recreate.

And Last But By No Means Least,

Ask Yourself …

What Would I

Do

If I Weren't

Afraid?

You'll

Make

The Right Decision.

Everyone Will BE Afraid At Some Time Or Another,

But No One Needs To <u>STAY</u> Afraid!

We Have Come To

The End

Of Our Time

Together,

For Now.

I Hope That You Will Choose To Be

Joyful

That You Took Some Time

To Be Aware Of,

And To Care For,

Yourself.

I Know I Am

Joyful

About That.

While Any One Of Us

Is Controlled By

Fear

None Of Us

Can Truly

Think And Feel

Freely.

And If You Feel

Fearless,

You Will Behave,

Fearlessly.

And Each Person You 'Touch'

In That State Of Mind

Will Touch Another

And So Forth…

So You Can Help

Many, Many People

By <u>Helping Yourself</u>

In A Constructive

Way,

Isn't That Fabulous?!

I Love That About

<u>You</u>!

Until We Meet Again,

I Wish You

Wisdom,

Productive Decision Making,

Love,

And

Magic!

The End…

And A Beginning,

For Endings

Always Are

You Know!

About the Author

Dr. Margaret Cochran has been an educator and professional therapist for more than 28 years.

Her background and experience have given her a unique perspective from which to provide help, insight and healing. With graduate degrees in Education, Social Work and Transpersonal Psychology she has worked with a wide variety of clients, both individual and organizational.

Dr. Cochran's professional goal is to facilitate constructive change. To assist people in viewing the world as a place of plenty rather than paucity; finding out what keeps people stuck in negativity and giving them the tools to achieve their dreams. She is fond of saying that, "Everyone is unique, valuable and special. Everything you do and don't do is important, everything you say and don't say is important and at the same time you need to put your big girl pants on and get over yourself!"

Dr. Cochran lives in the mountains of Northern California with her beloved husband and any number of magical creatures.

www.drcochran.com

CPSIA information can be obtained at www.ICGtesting.com
Printed in the USA
266709BV00001B/18/P